www.finishinglinepress.com

The Runaway Poems:
A Manual of Love

poems by

Gabriella Gutiérrez y Muhs

Finishing Line Press
Georgetown, Kentucky

The Runaway Poems: A Manual of Love

I dedicate my poems to all the runaway humans,
who could simply not remain in their surroundings;
wishing them safety, warmth and love.

It never stopped, this running. We were constant prey, and the hunters soon became big blurs: the police, the gangs, the junkies, the dudes on Garvey Boulevard who took our money, all smudged into one. Sometimes they were teachers who jumped on us Mexicans as if we were born with a hideous stain. We were always afraid. Always Running.

—Luis J. Rodríguez, Always Running

For my students, every morning I am whole.

I want to, daily, every morning pick up the pieces of me, left on my bed under my sheets. Complete, renewed unscathed, altered only by respect.
I want to be like my dog, immune to hate, lovingly strong. I want to be the woman my unsuspecting students expect, my runaway child expects, to look for . . .

ACKNOWLEDGMENTS

"Returning" has been published electronically in *Puerto del Sol.*
"In Pieces" and "Flight 491 (Lufthansa from Frankfurt to Madrid)" have been published in *Red Wheelbarrow.*

Publisher: Leah Maines

Editor: Christen Kincaid

Cover Art: Eric Muhs

Author Photo: Rati Saxena

Cover Design: Eric Muhs

Printed in the USA on acid-free paper.
Order online: www.finishinglinepress.com
also available on amazon.com

Author inquiries and mail orders:
Finishing Line Press
P. O. Box 1626
Georgetown, Kentucky 40324
U. S. A.

Table of Contents

The Araña Poem (Spider and I)

You and I,
we walk the trapeze,
life's tight rope of tragedy
we share
the fact
that we
may not
save our web
beyond today.

Swinging a run-away child

She played at the park
still virgin at heart
never imagining
She was swinging a runaway boy,
a "missing child" ten years ahead.

She innocently kissed him,
not yet knowing of betrayal.
Sure, her father had abandoned
her mother
And, not loved her enough
Her sister had preferred alcohol,
to her love
But, she was still
eating ignorance with peanut butter
not knowing
the well of unimagined tears
she would once outsource,
to another nation,
to her students,
her oblation
the world with—
Her son—she thought as she swung him higher
would always want her hug
her macaroni and cheese,
her huevos con chorizo,
her elevated love.
Her hugs, her milk,
the way she walked,
the tickles she provided
the warmth produced in him.
She was still ten years away
from future hell,
from the inside of a police station at 3am,
from the explanations to strangers of
Why he left:
"He thought we didn't love him enough,"
"he hung out with the wrong crowd,"
"he hates his big house,"
"he had never had friends, and wanted to be accepted,"
"he was swinging from the wrong tree,"

could not see us from there,
too high, swinging away.

Emmanuel

At six
you sat
almost lost in the beanbag
on the ground
in your first grade attire,
in the counselor's office.
Your beany eyes
would whistle at me
intermittently,
I letting her know
you had become
a cash cow for a second grader,
a fruit rollup cow
for the boy
who demanded your fruit rollups—
everyday—
or he would tease you
or he would push you
or he would bully your belly
your spirit,
put a dent in your mind,
a blue mark in your ego,
a social scab
would be planted in you,
in front of other boys.
But you would have none of that
standing up
for the author of your wound
we heard, the counselor and I your beanbag buried voice
defending your oppressor—"he has six brothers and sisters, where else could he
get fruit rollups?" all rolled up
in your shouting transparent justice.

Walkabout

Chamomile did not make you whole
as I suspected, my son.
It didn't cure the ache
of immigration:
Your grandfather's native ache,
Your great-great-grandfather's European ache,
You still had to go
on your urban Walkabout, my growth.
No, the chamomile, peppermint, mango, guava, cloves and cinnamon tea
I transfused into you
did not put you at ease.
The novena I prayed for,
for your restless nightmares,
didn't calm you.
The herbs, the prayers, the happy colors of your room,
the blessing by the curandero at the Zócalo last year
did not cure you,
the sweeping by the old Zapotec woman didn't feed you, my son
the picture of you, my friend took to the Virgin's Villa my dear, did nothing for
you.
Your nostalgia
was knee high deep, my love,
our cutting of your hair
did not purify you.
The toxins of your culture were far gone,
they had become part of your active blood
Huitzilopochtli—my son
my pieces have become whole
in your presence again
I, Coatlicue, have collected
resculpted, redesigned my heart into your head, your head into my heart,
oh my child God.

The Runaway

I.
Where did you run to
my poisoned limb?
Did they tell you to notice the value of black hoodies,
to follow the coarseness of TV programs,
to admire the dedication of hate towards elders, the value of being a criminal,
in a criminalized society, especially
for nonwhite men?

II.
Buses will never be the same—
Should we follow this one, does it contain our love, the creature that resulted from
the toys, the milk, the vegetables and apples we bought?

Does he know that sometimes buses are vehicles of fiction,
terror, miles and untruths—quarters that bite—
transfers that reroute the lives of tears
The lives of teens
who wish not to do the lawn after school, empty the trash from their bedrooms,
wash the cars with their pops,
flush the words from their phones.

III.
By the second day, my love,
we thought they had burned you alive,
for not stealing for them
for not telling us lies
for not turning us into your hoodlum friends' enemies.
How many days does it take
to change lanes
after signaling
on the road to adulthood?

Disappearances

They were not supposed to tell us where you were
your friends acquaintances and fans
your Facebook follies.
Watching the electronic circus of your life:
the girls you gave my jewelry to,
so they would like you,
those who could not value
Gold, my son,
could also not see how hard you shine,
not see how deep the well of your intelligence
subtracts
from being common, normal, useless—dim.

Returning

In my recurring dreams of you today I sent you to school, you were toothless and 7, but you kept returning home, like an unaddressed letter, a ticketless passenger, a nameless angel in front of Saint Peter

You, dressed "like an Indian" to you, which meant just you naked, walking around calmly beautifully Naked~pumpkin~naked! May your soul always come back home Naked~RE-TUNED

Dumbo Memories

You and I cuddled watching Dumbo,
which is about the love of a baby for his mom,
about the elephant who flies.
Not with wings, but with ears.
And you crying when the mother
is imprisoned
for defending Dumbo.
Taken away from me
I am, my love, imprisoned,
in life without your presence.
Please take the bars away,
my anguish must fly
in your wings *querido*.
It must not be buried,
but freed in what you
wish to become.
You the ears, who hear me
be, what you wish for in a mom.
Fly my love, fly my love
hear me be,
you
ears are for flying!

The Day I Lost My Calm in the Dog Park...

While the waves approached
the dog owners for approval
while they approximated
the launched balls
with plastic contraptions
for their dogs to fetch, exercise, dream,

While the balls got lost in Lake Washington
I realized that like the balls
my runaway son was lost,
but not lost
to all shores,
that he would like the balls
be brought back by the waves
because waves always return
what is not theirs
unlike bad relatives, sometime friends, and colleagues

Waves, never taking forever
unlike death, time, or fire
waves will return him to a shore where he is
safe, loved, capable of being
the child I raised,
the man his father models,
the brother his brother holds,
in the heat of a constant phase
of love.

Sierra

No you are not a tree, or a mountainous drawing—
Sierra Maderos—a female from Oregon
you appear on USA Today Aug. 21-23, 2009
smilingly I carry your newspaper face in my purse
know your DOB: Oct 25, 1993
your "biracial" description by heart
know that in your brown eyes
someone found a way to convince
you on June 24, 2007—
St. John's day—
that you were better off away
from home—or took you—or killed you—
or you escaped for whatever reason
and now you are another "missing"
1-800-the lost child
in the National Center for Missing and
Exploited Children's archive.
You thicken the tree of this Sierra of loss
your face represents danger, tenderness,
love, sadness, compassion and anger
all tightly wound around the word missing
a forest of feelings lined up like toothpicks in
the lives of those who
have lost Sierras,
those who clamor for sustainability.

Corners

In the corner of her bed
she found inspiration.
Corners always turning
the other way.
She understood them.

She swam imaginary laps
uninterruptedly, thinking of her son,
corner child,
cornered away—in the
corners of her mind
by bullies, strangers, children unloved.
The pool was situated for her
nearest to her imagination
the profound pool of her love.
Imagine,
no one knew the reason for the ocean
in her brown eyes,
the peculiar cost of smiling
from birth on,
the slow cost of headaches,
documenting health,
trying to stay one day ahead of diseases,
the charge for having such a good life
all at once.

Love Is a Luxury

A minute in flight every day
upon which a memory settles

love is a luxury says the 8 year old boy,
who knows his grandmother
may not have another birthday
with which to love him

love is the luxury of rubbing ones eyes upon it
before we stare at
the eternal moment we created

the man who limps and reminds me of my mother is a luxury

and the drunk who begs to never drink again
is my father, the luxury of his yearning withstanding

what else could we become?

Domingos

It is not what we lose each Sunday that we fear,
it is what we don't see that mesmerizes us:
The post office closed, no happy person about to mail a present that makes him
generous.
No mother saying goodbye as if for the first and last time,
one hundred and eighty one mornings a year.
No mailman dropping by the mail box of people he will never see,
whose faces he scrutinizes through the letters they receive.

It is not what we lose each Sunday that we fear:
the goodbye kisses
the rushed affection floating by
the lattes we give ourselves on weekday mornings: a settlement for loneliness
the hugs we hug
the empty pens we find that we must toss away—inkless forever,
the intimate mornings with our cars,
the conversations of commuting spirits,
the trust that we are in fact capable of living one more day away from those we
love.

It is the loneliness of Sundays,
oftentimes,
without the holy spirit
the Sunday paper---
the exercise week---
the talk with ourselves
in which we lose
one of the people
we carry inside

Freeway Man

"Within utilitarian ethics,
sighs are not counted
gazes dissipate
smiles are forgotten, squandered away
and Sundays are a waste.
It is within the confines of materialism
that we bag up
forgiveness,
dispense smiles in health pills
weigh the beauty of nature for proper measurements,
quantify the breaths of air it costs us to say hello.
We use others and have them use us
in multiple manuable manners
we document,
we surrender"
recited by Freeway man
to the shelter boys,
at the shelter for teens who feel unsafe,
but mostly who feel unloved
in the way they wish
to be loved
by their parents.

Filial Encounter

As I gave him a dollar
I touched him, purposefully, my car driving
off—the light had turned—
our only encounter
would be that of a mother
remembering her son
and loving the man on the corner with a sign
because he had a mother—somewhere
who reminded her
of her self
—in pain—in love.

Sending Bundles

They sometimes contain powerful feelings:
socks, pants, toothpaste, books, letters, memories, pictures,
chocolate, pan dulce,
a long noodle of love that connects like an umbilical cord
all coiled up inside a paper box, 14 years long
14 years of my love.
Writing letters to a son who should be here
is not an ordinary thing.
Maybe they would ask for a blood donation if they knew that the straw that makes
this pen write in blood
is hollow.
Blood only circulates
in empty receptacles,
and I am full of you, my love.

The Hard Love of a Dog

Because he lived in the street,
he knows how to ask for meanings without words,
how to nurse milk out of concrete,
water out of wood,
how to play with the same love differently,
how to sniff out the unbearable endings.

Chewing to think,
an empty bowl speaks for your needs
Chewing the thing that most threatens your survival
starving to understand from within—the acute sentiments of life.

The lickings of love unlimited,
the layered significance of bone gnawing,
endless communications of sighs
and whimpers,
all signed by your saliva.

Another version

No, it wasn't millionaires who sent them away,
it was not selfish parents
shipping off their
progeny
unto others
to raise.
It was hard working workers, teachers, friends of friends,
who believed the page would turn, from their 16 year old
cocaine addicts'
indulgent, self-victimizing
self-criminalizing
techies in trouble,
who in fact sometimes,
unknowingly tortured
their parents for attention,
bottomless loads of endless attention,
for playing Hollywoodish lives
on real life TV.

Pink Sands in Utah

You rolled, ran, yelled, sang
like the pet by your side, brotherhood and paws.

You listened to the music
of the sand,
to the screaming of the Spanish, French and German Tourists,
to the running of the dog,
to the justice of the sand,
you were a normal
15 year old boy—
all of us happy through
pink colored glass.

Living in the moment,
living for the instant
in pink
the day before we
returned you to your school rules
army-like system
scheduled meals and morning
alarm clock risings,
supervision voices of experts
against the voices of young lies—
indomitable tales.

The sand stayed in my shoes,
your pink sand laughter still falls
inside my time clock of you.

Nature is kind.

Bryce Canyon

We left you
with your teachers,
supervisors,
made up—
friends
of made up stories.

The distinct
edges
of the parallel
columns
erected
towards hope
at Bryce Canyon, the layered truth
disconnected from reality
all made up of solid dirt
beautiful dirt
dirt of dead ancestors
who collect themselves
cautiously
to comfort the pain
of wounded parents
on the solitary stretcher
of teenagedom.

The Homeless Shelter Benefit

That evening the reading for homeless teenagers your dad and I
unknowingly attended.
It was there I cried a full container of bottled water for you, my son.
Listen to the stories of injustice—
runaways who had suffered
running off from worthless parents:
drug addicts and all sorts of selfish characters
their inkfull tears they spilled
telling—of their junky parents—
their hateful stepdads—their alcoholic mothers— their abandoned single
dads—who worked odd hours
irritated by economic deeds— who had unjustly beat them
emotionally—none of them
Us—my son.

¿What was it that we didn't do for you?
¿Could we have possibly not loved you enough?
¿What is enough, my son? What is enough?
¿Did we soil your path with our love?

Rosina and her dead and imprisoned sons

With our privilege of professionals, we pulled you away
from fears, hoodlums, parents, haters, abused children who could
no longer forgive children
abusive of other children
future junkies, haters, workers
we 007ed you like hawks
ah, our middle class
privilege, another
chance at hope and future
In traffic,
I cried out loud
for Rosina—
made faces at commuters
with my smeared mascara—
prescribed eyeshadow
evil red lipstick
inconsolably
I cry for Jorge, Luis, Carlos, José, Pete
Rosina's five children
melted away by guns
at the green valley apartments
the government housing
where the gang territory of every gang member
was only inside his apartment
where boys had no choice but to fight
and where 007 movies were as foreign as most resources—
a checking account, a running car—
money in the bank—
a retirement plan, a college fund.

Your father lifts you away
from the danger—
sleeps you in the back of the SUV,
drives you to another territory—
where Facebook—
phone wires, iPod, internet
can't snake you back into mistakes, ingratiate you with criminals
where "open campuses" with bus passes
don't take you away
in buses
without stops
where Zestos like hamburger joints
don't sell pot across the street from your middle-class high school
where man is not against nature
and nature is not against man—
away from the wires
that have been choking you
into truancy and terror—
away because
we can
take you away
to make you ours.
I cry for Rosina
away forever
from her sons.

Nimble Fingers

Unlike your cousins,
products of the maquiladoras,
the border, poverty, immigration,
factories where watches get made
by nimble fingers,
we all won the lottery of social class.

Your fingers are
nimble tourists of pleasure,
triumphant thumbs of the future,
trained by gameboy,
your fingers
do the dialing
of divertissement—
your body enjoys
a resetting of the past,
the nimble pleasures of plastic buttons
being raised on the high road.

A rewind,
we are able to amass through our social class
with our nimble fingers, your father and I worked the system
erase,
create a new character
allow
you
to try again
to become yourself.

In a space
on the filters of love.

An Electronic Boy

Trees sometimes go unheard by your lines,
no home more home than home for the runaway,
unfettered wishes still run out of his detachable wires—
he leaves in strains of Facebook only to go around the block of reality.
The runaway has finally
downloaded himself into the present, without a wire
his wires are plugged into
our souls
our ears can hear his connections
our hearts can beat his image
we now have the possibility of
running away together
electronically
crossing wires with
hands.

You Are Joaquín

You are Joaquín, my love—
you are the biracial embodiment of love
I will not allow for buses, cars, trains, airplanes, or unloved pains
to take you away
from the arboretum of your life.

We did not, my dear,
learn to cross lines
to pick onions in Los Baños,
artichokes in Castroville,
to make watches in Chicago,
pick apples in Washington
for you to easily
leave the path of remembrance.

We did not, my dear, divest from South Africa,
learn to speak English
to vote for Obama
or the language of Cornel West or, my dear,
the language of my culture
to end up in concrete.

You can never run away
from the culture we grafted on your memory,
the food of touch your grandma already invested in our account,
the celebrations of love we placed in your portfolio
from birth on.

Generations of our people would be undone.

The program of your runaway path, my dear, is deleted
because we're not done evolving.
My insurance prevails.

My love for you, dear, is my pre-existing condition.

Your Silver Lining Is Not Limited to Me

Because I love you
on a deserted island that is life
I will write to you a letter
with a roll of toilet paper.
I will write on a cloud for you like the Chinese women
brocaded their lovers'
shirts, at night.
To not hurt you, I will write of my love for you, on dirt.
I will mail to you an archive
of newly felt kisses through the internet
of my heart.
Until you know that stars
are the shadowed versions of your palpitating words.
You are the ring on the broken finger
that holds it together,
your silver lining is not limited to me.

Rapture

Come—measure me in my tears of joy.
In the landscape of love
I am immensely small and terribly deep
I want to freeze the road of your pain
I want to bury your feelings into an envelope of forgetfulness
fullness
forgiveness.
Give me your past loss,
I will fill it with wonder,
file it in the amazement of phantoms,
carry it to the flower offerings of May in a small town,
in a foreign country perfume it,
in the distance of absence,
email it to God.

Fallen Apple

On days of thorn,
I am dead in the vine,
fallen from the fruit tree
rotten in a pile of apples
that will become cider

Good things do come from rot,
I must remember
my defiled father's dreams
ended when he was six,
he drank and drank
alcohol
his favorite costumed life
the sins of the grandfather are the sins of the grandson,
but they are not sins, yes tragedies
and sometimes don't contain a path,
or a bubble in which to write ostentatiously
gleaming thoughts about
how we are incarcerated
in the sadness of the street children
our parents were,
long ago.

A Banana Pendulum

"Bananas, like people, they are scanned,
but their territorial accent
does not dissuade the consumer from consuming."

"Unlike people, we consume them
without accusing them of being immigrants."

¿What could my son hang on his neck with which no one will ask him what he is,
or where he's from, in Seattle?

¿Could we wire up a chile, a tortilla, a cactus, or a bean, and dangle it from his
fluctuating identity?

¿Can he have already wallowed himself on a flower tortilla to make himself a
bicultural burrito appealing to all, yet acceptable to none?

¿Dónde dejaste a tu abuela? (Where's your grandma?)

Her image levitates behind you, like a mountain of un-shattered hope.
She would have never let you carry her,
she knows about the loads of obligation,
they always drag...

Where did you leave us?

After years of holding our breaths, rural grandma held us up with her titanium
hips,
her undying smile, her immigrant hunger,
her infamous title of: "fastest line worker,"
for Watsonville Canning,
her sustaining, unscathed heart, palpitating tirelessly, like prayer, defending you:

He's ok, at least he did not steal our cows... he only left for a while...

In Pieces

We all are pieces of pieces.
In my purse, I carry
the pieces of people I can't see,
a paper list of my dreams,
a barrette, lipstick, pen
they dignify me.

I file in my wallet a jr. high school picture of a son,
reminds me of the spirit he was
back then, before the lion
on the picture, ate his face.

A high school picture of my other son,
that wants me to hug him.

The parking ticket I enjoy never paying.

I carry a wallet of purposeful years,
a wallet of cards that were once valid,
a dollar from the 1950's
a man once told me was worth four,
the stamps I will use
to write the letters
where
I describe my life as I wish it were,
pieces of white lies
that like clouds keep me centered,
I carry.

Flight 491 (Lufthansa from Frankfurt to Madrid)

In the air, I have no relatives,
culture, problems or future

I REST

I cannot hate or love
I am perfect, whole
one suitcase and a bag
a passport, computer and phone
an agenda and a soul full of hope
no way to touch or be touched
the freedom of innocence and inconsequence.

On this plane there are no fences or choices of permanence.

On this plane choices are few, rare, counted: peanuts or pretzels.

On the air, a bird am I, inside another manmade dream, in the air.

On the plane, I rest from housework, chores, emails and promises,
forget we are wearing down, with every nocturnal gaze,
with every day on earth, we grow a new tree ring,
with every passing ship, cloud or pool below.

On the plane, we rule over a world of movement, only birds away...

Only the Pillow Swims to My Water

I would like to blanket
those who sing with their teeth on a snowy morning,
the parents of the activist who is run over by a
tractor
I would like to blanket
the man who wishes to hate his co-workers, and drink
cold coffee at night
the poet who wrote his last poem before the war
the shopping teenager who isn't happy otherwise
the mother from the 50's who sends clippings to her
children because she can't talk to them without
commands.
The alcoholic who runs to the liquor store on a cold

night after a three hour AA meeting.
¿Could love wash their feet?
¿clean their tormented ears?
¿remove the calcite deposits from their eyes?
¿Or could a song, wake them up, caulk their wounds,
return them to the shelter of their mind?

To Thresh a Vice

undress the husks of time
unbaste the soul of your ancestors
unbraid the unnumbered chains of shame
forgive the echo of misdirected words
breathe in the silence of your ancestors, your enemies
flail your insecurities
let alcohol less dreams boil in passion
kiss yourself in the heart
for surviving
yourself

billboards

until light comes
we remain like brail to a baby
we might be blind, and not know it...
further than thunder,
undetermined yet,
by their ways,
with laughter, appreciation, love,
we are lit
someone understands that our message won't be read in the darkness
of politics,
until light comes
and blood retains
the remainders of memory...

Four thoughts that will ground you at work, for the rest of your life, that will take you to the hope well, when you are dry

I
Without knowing of a shelter, secure a set of people
who will with their sight rescue you.

II
Take your heart out of the cage
to breathe the oxygen of forgiveness once a day,
open the front and the back door at once.
Liberate your spirit in letting sadness and rancor only pass through your newly
waxed floors and corridors, like a meteorite, without time for soiling your soul.

III
If the skeleton of the past awaits our fleshing of reality,
our image of beneficence to others needs to be sketched,
until our body becomes part of the common good.

IV
Imagine. The unscathed sky of dreams
seems to wrap around your unblemished thoughts,
like a winter coat in Antarctica. Create.

Additional Acknowledgements

I thank my Mother Socorro Favela for her unconditional strength, widsom, support and love, my husband Eric Muhs for his music and loyalty, my son Enrico Muhs for nurturing me, giving me love, and for ALWAYS being oh so wise. For my Tello Muhs, because he has done so much for so many, who could not remain, and might not have thanked him. You and yours are my inspiration for this collection. For all the young homeless I see every day....I wish my words could be your home....I would like to thank Leah Maines and Finishing Line Press, Amanda Westby, my wonderful assistant at Seattle University that I was able to fund thanks to a Dean's Fellowship for a research assistantship in Arts and Sciences. In my daily life I thank all my cousins and other relatives, especially my mother in law Debbie Radbill, and also my cousins Ofelia Fabela and Ruth Gutiérrez, who have always loved me unconditionally.

I would not be able to remain unscathed and loving without the support of those who have shared many subjectivities with me, my colleagues and friends. My words will heal because of all of you. I am sorry if I miss any one person: MaryAntoinette Smith, Kathy Cook, Jodi O'Brien, Jeanette Rodriguez, Connie Anthony, Maria Carl, Victoria Kill, Paulette Kidder, Christina Roberts, Catherine Punsalan, Sharon Suh, Sabina Neem, Teresa Jones, Melissa Morisi, Rati Saxena, Arlene Lee, Steven Bender, Tayyab Mahmud, Carmen González, Sharon Cumberland, Sharon Callahan, Jessica Ludescher-Imanaka, Nalini Iyer, John Fraire and Martina Iñiguez, Deb Busman, Rhonda Woods, Thorne Clayton-Falls, Edward Salazar, Grace Chang, Kari Lerum, Shari Dworkin and Jesús Rosales, Ben Olguín, Norma E. Cantú, Helena María Viramontes, Rebecca Burciaga, María Esther Quintana, Ken Weisner, Donna Miscolta, Wendy Call, especially for Bob Flor, Kathleen Alcalá, Sofiana Olivera, Xánath Caraza and Catalina Cantú .Thank you Guadalupe Vega McKeithen for spending time with my mother. Thanks to my compadres Dan Goldberg, Dan Pickard, Winfield Hobbs and Alex Flores, for being there for us, and our boys. For my comadres Graciela, Guadalupe and Martha Vega, and Pedro and Mercedes Martín. For our Seattle friends Anne Marie Peterson and George Donovan, Vanessa Castañeda and my cousins Remedios Favela, Lily and Adela Lechuga, María Elena Rocha, Conchita Rivera, Joel Frías and his family, as well as all my other cousins.

Always for my professors and professor friends: Yvonne Yarbro-Bejarano, Mary Louise Pratt, Francisco Lomelí, Annabelle Rea, Lauro Flores, Don Luis Leal, Sheilah Serfaty Wilson, Bettina Aptheker, Adrienne Rich, Lorna Dee Cervantes, Christina Herrera, Susana Gallardo, Rebeca Burciaga, Cheryl Matías, Aurora Chang, Isiaah Crawford, Larissa Mercado-López, Mare Blocker, Rachel Mayo and especially Shirley Flores Muñoz.

For my ex-students, now friends;
Marianne Mork, Aldo Reséndiz, Noemi Natividad, Gabriela Boyle, Rachael Brown, Brenda Trejo, Emma Jornlin and Monica Reyes, and especially Veronica Eldredge and Olga Díaz.

CPSIA information can be obtained
at www.ICGtesting.com
Printed in the USA
LVOW11s0902260317
528474LV00001B/42/P